hardPressed Dual Poets Reader: One

hardPressed Dual Poets Reader: One

Sheila Mannix

Nathan Spoon

Published by hardPressed poetry, Ireland

http://hardpressedpoetry.blogspot.com/

hardpressedpoetry@gmail.com

You built you framing you are multiplying © Sheila Mannix 2017

My Name is Gretchen Merryweather © Nathan Spoon 2017

This edition © hardPressed poetry 2017

ISBN: 978-1-872781-07-5

All rights reserved
No part of this publication may be reproduced in any form or by any means without prior permission of the publisher.

You built you framing you are multiplying

Sheila Mannix

Material: Sade's *Dialogue entre un prêtre et un moribond* translated by Google into Irish & from Irish into English

The site became lethal

the veil of illusion

that tearing

man seduces the cruel picture

of errors and vices

multiple disorders

the weaker and stronger person

Enjoy the happy remorse for the sky

by intervention you understand me

here created by nature

very sharp taste

very passions strong

the effects prove to be

only the first views

All because of adequately

recognized omnipotence

I made poor use of the faculties

I have sometimes resisted

blinded by the absurdity of the system

I fought them

I have harvested in flower

when I might make a full crop of fruit

You built you framing you are multiplying

I destroy I simplify

you add errors errors

the I all fight

it must be immediate reports

understanding

is a necessary

demand

You do not understand

you do not understand

you cannot provide

any reasonable argument

in a word

nothing above the limits

of the human mind

or chimera or worthlessness

I would be a fool to believe it

a fool

Do not expect anything from me

I'm going to do the obvious

I will get to my senses

stop powerless

I think the sun as I see it

I see it as meeting

all kinds of flammable

a periodic walk

a physical process

as simple as electricity

Understand the worker

lay on the item

you have done me a service

by building your dream

you disturbed mind

you were not lit

I do not owe you

places recognition

machine moving at will

Discomfort I have tumbled

calm and philosophy

scare your sophistry

a fear without reproof

irritate without improve

a result of the companies

willing to train me

of views and their needs

essential vices and virtues

inspired I want

I got shipped anyway

To laws only reason

our human inconsistency

everything is needed worldwide

everything is fixed

fix everything all-powerful hand

the powder ignites the fire

the necessary things

without providing

for anything

it is useless

Great probability is not zero need

zero is a chimera

I do not need any other reasoning

the certainty of uselessness

Fanaticism and imbecility

these trends have money

if prodigious

the table is terrible

in my opinion

a ridiculous system

cult

daydreams

snake

absurdities

god

armies

sects

heresy

The most normal of all cunning

equal the impostors

lend me your comments

prophecy

miracles

martyrs

all evidence recorded in history

I have more force than any historical facts

transmitted by historians

the simplest policy may be evidence

About your miracles

they do not convince me

what is outside could pass for a miracle

(many dare to say

this is precisely the time

it is broken)

you preach empire

in the heart

the man had his work

the sanctuary for his act

the same law

a way irresistible

etched in everyone

from one end of the globe

to another

Resisting the inclination to worship

I see instead a universe

as many gods as countries

the art of imposing

on the people

punishable by the state

(wise to delete

maxims may be dangerous

the government is one)

Your mind is not rain

pierce the thick of fate

the system can be better

than willing numerous penalties

eternity of rewards

of nothingness

not scared

me I see nothing

so comforting and simple

absolute nothingness

in front of my eyes

perpetual generations

and regenerations of nature

Nothing perishes

nothing destroyed the world

you can bring your improved system

the system of freedom

invented for the manufacture

so favourable to your dreams

light scaffolding near the boiler

requires perfect balance

We can be guilty

no more than that

darting wasp sting

comes to your skin

The law condemns sword justice

remoteness or terror

sterile remorse

its effect is vain

could not save us

nor repair

it is absurd to fear

worldwide adjacent

know the escape

do not give up

the pleasure

to be happy and to do

that's the way

nature gives you

to double your existence

or expansion

Pleasure

the most expensive

of articles

my whole life

I wanted my arms full

I booked the time

to hand

to try to forget

with my sample

all the vain sophistries

of superstition

the fools errors

of hypocrisy

nature failed to explain

My Name is Gretchen Merryweather

Nathan Spoon

For the Family Gerridae

Adios

i have never   met a stranger

who wasn't a friend.   have,

i confess,   never used a
contraction

in a contraception   +

there is the matter   of

whatever   was is a yester-
second

ago.   welcome out.

Elastic Sand

here in the city of freshly
minted

dangers try when you

to get away, you find

you get a wave

all of the sails unfurl

billowing in the direction

anticipated. those of us

you leave   behind show
hands.

we   do not remain

Congratulations

it is up there uhuh   it was not
except

when it is see it   down there

sorry you missed when   it
passed before

your eye   when it bit

your retina.   priorly now

you go tell   me wow about it

America

i need   assault fam

to protect   my gun.

High Five

certain words are spelled
correctly. you

are not missing a thing. leeks
are there

in the kitchen behold to that
with ever what

before caused so do not put
your

sass here hey hey.

Hot Spot

i live in a country   at war i
don't know

with i don't know seven   i
don't

muslim know countries.   no

non-muslim   countries gus

anti-muslim rhetoric
smothers me

it a lot   others talk like we
walk.

Umbrella

she's on her   phone wanted

to catch up with   and let you
know

she's out the done door   and
now

we will always   know exactly

what she said   minus

the words whatever   she's
saying

Fighead

you picked   just like

the 50,000 lb.   sack

of assholes   you are

the ocelot   out of

rimbaud's   nose

Raincoat

up in a bird   a tree inverted

tiny ivy desert its.   is tickled

through to the mustard   of
spies

and an   envelop containing

a postcard with   a message
that read

if you can read this   if is it
blank

Accordion Beast

why you sashayed   across my
sassafras

because   a got dug hole
flippantly into

the situation of our   shared
circumstances

flinging along neither   of us
was both

wrong we instead   was both
starred

right and ripe as　　　　　　watery
pickles. i

wanted dark arts　　　　　　wisely to
apologize

you as you you torch　　　　　touched
my cloud sigh.

*

flocking to buy out　　　　　me and
casual the lozenges

you and really, gus,　　　　　really do
you have to throw

your overcoat　　　　　around like
that. especially when

you know the corresponding crow
always

is always watching from   just
behind the front

of the neighborly hedges   our
neighbors

keep pledging to find. before
you think you

before you grind you   my to
dislocated knuckles

so glacial!   the tongue tho to
rubble runs

*

bunched hands   do up
crumble my

lunch wizard   whisper +
hammocks

keep over actually and   plate
my table

absurdly + broadly   only. only
relatively

speaking and gum glum.
remember where

the piece that moon of fell
and real now how

*

precisely					hi how's

everybody's					lots

*

nobody argues this with me
until it's worsered

until it's diamonded					so
pearled. words

are nothing much when something
gets

more said. when i cry a lot
look who cares

again. took out   the sled and
again across

the downhill field goes us
went here. so there

is that to be   eventually
oblivious and proud

which only. if ever
snowwoman arms

embracing   broke open the joy
make of winter's

He Dropped It

later he altered   his while
chewing

around a stick   of gum and

invent to how   along the shore

3,000 feet down   and wearing

a pair of googly eyes   giant's
eyes

do not fear of mine   as a
maple.

Prattical

prattles a lot   flips the over
sofa

fights for   social justice real

around real cyberscapes
smartered.

due being to head-fed   + heart-
led.

me the   radical loves the
different in you there.

unless you be oystered
coloured tater tot mean

and follow tweeting   the
tater's what saying

Mask/Math

i'm coming over there			to wet
my beak on

that goofy grapefruit			we all
collaborated on

last century + if as			you recall
wait a bit

also before also crawling			my
pants leg also

whittle			while you whistle a
little, gus, k

Ur Adjunct

her a heart   hole full

of moustaches   which he

complained about   and didn't

mind. look, he said,   the scene

is reflecting off   your
sunglasses

which is what   happens at
night.

Cute Boots

oh god the rockets   are my off

in mid air   again somebody

must produce   the biggest
amount

of guns gus to keep   us in the
popped

slot. otherwise hell   the
russians

will rise where we   thimble
off

In a Pit

apparently a number   is a
word

is a mask   is a person

who forgot to put   a cap on
her druthers

salty   as carmel road butter.

it happens   as he was thinking

about how before she   knew
which did

My Name Is Gretchen Merryweather

all the images repeating   in
words your mind

are all the same repeating   in
her mind. she

is we. + i am   trying to fall
asleep right precisely

wow   and nobody languages
these days

aside from the same newbies
who relentlessly

loiter under one leafy counter
of the candy store.

*

[phone audio]

everywhere's grieved   my
moonlight is angry

before you tomorrow me any
boulders

think how   delicate jumble
hipster marvel you

lost your sock and now   who
gives a fuck how

it's situated when if   eye-
bitten you strain over

*

if when ever this is by
anybody ever read have

a wine full of flowers.   before
the long balloon

carries   a short echo back
across the adjacent

hollow. if you puff in a frenzy
so that nobody

will notice + glass   in the mass
and overturned

edoxus that's why certainly
so much is deepening

is the flailing root of what is
again is present.

well no huh at least is the be safe count
words is

so go go go go go if   taste can
goodness anywhere

*

pliable and strong it is   of a
this ago tho.

and so   wondered what the
were are

butter-knifing around what he
thought she

thought   in the blanket-dazzle
of period foolery.

and just as period the spies settled in
for lovely

*

across and a path might night
a hologram axis

leaning left then right then
left then right

is the way to   get together
some monsterly

equipoise while looking of course
both ahead

and behind in the advice
swaggering tsunami.

then in the first february week
all robins all

returned at once until   by
wearing a dunce cap.

if the them of now   bends to
demonize the oddest

possible target   the would be
better than would

be seemingly everest at least or
the goddamn andes

XO

my revenge body   of course is

aways resexualizing   a lot

otherwise i would not be
shiny

and a scrappy   vanity mirror

it's minor now   like the you i
liked

upon a once   time. damn

how fine i am   see, you, i am
fine

Excuse Me

as the kind of person   who
had once

opinions, let   me tell you what
i think.

your's is the kind of table   we
all did

read about in fables.   now i am
ever

never able to cut to   some
chased point.

point chases me.   which what
do you see

when where stopped we
below spoken falls

Runes

ruining my ruin by looking

for snakes under stones

around my pond boat i want to

nap some more. the sky is

remember blue. if you do,

everywhere's shore you can

squint for   as you snail echo
what

gives to   live. you are called

samuel   and you are heard.

Friendship Cereal

do not hassle me, you. i'm a v
v

well-behaved and markedly
intellectual-ish

man-baby. i will crumble
exactly the way

a blade of grass crumbles
under wind

or if not wind then stratified
cork. yes,

everything you do tickles my
fancy well

so i srsly   do not mind. it's so
srsly fine.

i'm good, golden,   non-
goosed, unfucked,

srsly srsly so so so   super
duper fine.

Hello Again

this is boilerplate robotics
with a wig on it

a baker's dozen············that keeps
hounding around

into your blood············when you can
no longer keep

your eyes open even while some drone
pays barley

Sheila Mannix lives in Cork. Recent work has appeared in *Tripwire: a journal of poetics* (USA), *ZARF*, *Tears in the Fence*, *Shearsman* magazine (UK) and *gorse* (Ireland). Her first poetry chapbook *female corpse* was published by Smithereens Press in March 2017.
www.smithereenspress.com

Nathan Spoon is a bookseller at Parnassus Books. His publications include *Oxford Poetry*, *Mantis*, *Reflections* (Yale Divinity School), *From the Lighthouse* and *X-Peri*. He's been anthologized in *What Have You Lost?* (HarperCollins) and is the recipient of a Tennessee Williams Scholarship to the Sewanee Writers' Conference and an alumnus of the Home School. He is the Associate Editor of *X-Peri* and a faculty member for the 2017 Modernist Social Network seminar series at the University of Pennsylvania.

www.ingramcontent.com/pod-product-compliance
Lightning Source LLC
Chambersburg PA
CBHW020021050426
42450CB00005B/577